Firefighters
Then and Now

Melissa A. Settle, M.Ed.

Contributing Author
Jill K. Mulhall, M.Ed.

Associate Editor
Christina Hill, M.A.

Assistant Editor
Torrey Maloof

Editorial Director
Emily R. Smith, M.A.Ed.

Project Researcher
Gillian Eve Makepeace

Editor-in-Chief
Sharon Coan, M.S.Ed.

Editorial Manager
Gisela Lee, M.A.

Creative Director
Lee Aucoin

Illustration Manager
Timothy J. Bradley

Designers
Lesley Palmer
Debora Brown
Robin Erikson
Zac Calbert

Project Consultant
Corinne Burton, M.A.Ed.

Publisher
Rachelle Cracchiolo, M.S.Ed.

Teacher Created Materials
5301 Oceanus Drive
Huntington Beach, CA 92649-1030
http://www.tcmpub.com
ISBN 978-0-7439-9371-5
© *2007 Teacher Created Materials, Inc.*
Reprinted 2012

Table of Contents

Neighborhood Heroes

Firefighters (fiy-uhr-FIY-tuhrz) are people who are trained to put out fires. They help people in many ways. Firefighters **rescue** (RES-kyoo) people and animals in trouble. It is hard work.

⬆ Firefighters work hard to protect others.

🔼 Both men and women work as firefighters.

History of Fighting Fires

It is hard to put out a fire. But, it was even harder a long time ago. When there was a fire back then, people would form a long line. The line stretched from the fire to water. The people filled buckets with water. Then, they passed the buckets down the line. The person closest to the fire threw the water on the fire. It did not work very well.

▲ A fireman pulling a fire wagon

▲ Firefighters fight a big fire in 1850.

Later, George Washington ordered the first fire truck. It was just a wagon. But, it was a big help. This made it easier to get water to the fire. Horses usually pulled the early fire wagons. Sometimes, men had to pull the wagons.

An Unhappy Cow

In 1871, the city of Chicago burned to the ground. People think that a cow started the fire. She kicked over a lantern (LAN-tuhrn). Then, the barn caught on fire. And, the fire spread.

The city of Chicago on fire in 1871 ➡

Men training to ➡ be firefighters.

A Hard Job to Get

It is not easy to become a firefighter. They have to pass a written test. They also have to show that they are strong and in good shape.

Then, they must learn all about the job. They watch the real firefighters work. And, they practice using the tools. They have to prove that they have learned all of the skills that they need. If they do, they can become firefighters.

🔺 Firefighters have to train very hard.

Children Fighting Fires

Long ago, you could have been a firefighter. Children helped fight fires. They carried empty buckets for the men and women to fill with water.

◀ Two firefighters carry this lady to safety.

A Special Suit

Firefighters use many tools to help people.

Firefighters wear special **uniforms** (YOO-nuh-forms). These clothes help keep them safe from heat and smoke. Gloves protect their hands. Thick boots keep their feet dry.

Firefighters wear helmets on their heads. They wear masks on their faces. The masks hook up to special tanks they wear on their backs. The tanks are full of air to help them breathe.

In 1855, uniforms did not protect firefighters very well.

Covering Coat

A firefighter's coat is called a turnout coat. It is made of special thick cloth. These coats are great protection. They keep out fire and water.

The Tools They Need

Firefighters use many tools to fight fires. One important tool is a fire hose. Firefighters use these to spray water on fires. Some hoses are small and some are very big.

Sometimes firefighters use **crowbars**. These are used to open locked doors. Firefighters also use axes to break open walls. And, they use radios to talk to each other.

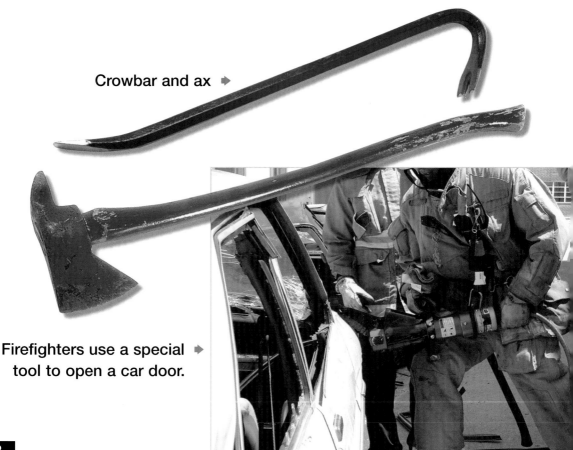

Crowbar and ax ➡

Firefighters use a special ➡
tool to open a car door.

▲ An early snorkel truck

A Snorkel Truck

There is a special type of fire truck. It is called a **snorkel** (SNORE-kuhl) **truck**. It can send a water hose way up in the air to fight a fire. A firefighter works the hose from the ground.

▲ A snorkel truck today sprays water on a fire.

Home Away from Home

Firefighters work many hours in a row. They have to wait to see if they will need to go to a fire. They wait at a place called a **fire station** (STAY-shuhn). This is where they park their trucks and keep their tools.

Often, firefighters have to spend the night at work. They need to be ready to help if there is a fire in the middle of the night. The fire station has beds and a kitchen.

At the end of a long **shift**, the firefighters go home.

◀ Firefighters work all night. Here, they rush to a fire early in the morning.

◀ Firefighters keep their uniforms ready at all times. When they need to leave, they jump in and go!

Time to Make Tasty Treats

Firefighters spend a lot of time at the fire station. They pass some of that time by cooking. They learn to make tasty meals. There are even many special cooking contests just for firefighters.

Not All Fire Trucks Are Engines

Most firefighters drive or ride in fire trucks. There are many types of fire trucks. Some fire trucks pump water or foam to help fight fires. The engine (EN-juhn) is what makes the pump work. So, they are called **fire engines** not fire trucks.

Other trucks have ladders on them. These ladders are very long. They help when people are trapped. Firefighters climb the ladders and help people down.

⬆ Ladder trucks lift firefighters above fires.

▲ A horse-drawn fire
engine from the
early 1900s

Out of the Way!

Firefighters hurry to get to
fires as quickly as they can.
That is why their trucks
have lights and **sirens** (SI-
ruhnz). These let other
drivers know that a fire
truck is coming. Drivers
know to get out of the way.

◄ Firefighters
enter a burning
building by
climbing a
tall ladder.

17

A Firefighter Needs Help

Many people help firefighters. When there is a fire, you can call 9-1-1 for help. The **dispatcher** (dis-PACH-uhr) calls the firefighters. This person tells the firefighters where to go.

Firefighters need help when people are hurt in a fire. So, they call the **paramedics** (pair-uh-MED-iks). These people have medical training. They help people who are hurt. Then, they take them to a hospital.

This woman is answering a 9-1-1 call.

◀ Paramedics work with firefighters to save people.

A Firefighter's Best Friend

A long time ago, horses used to pull fire trucks. Dogs called **dalmatians** (dal-MAY-shuhns) helped them. A dog would run beside or between the horses to keep them safe. Then, the dog would guard the trucks during the fire. Many fire stations still have dalmations as pets today.

A Different Kind of Fire

Not all fires are house fires. Some fires burn in forests. Lightning causes many fires. But, some fires start when people do not put out their campfires. These fires move very quickly. They can burn large areas of land.

▼ Forest fires spread very quickly.

Some firefighters get special training to fight forest fires. They are called smoke jumpers or hot shots. Helicopters (hel-ih-KOP-tuhrz) drop them right into the middle of a fire. It can be dangerous.

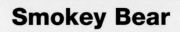

Smokey Bear

The Forest Service wanted people to be more careful when they were camping. So, they made up a cartoon bear. His name is Smokey Bear. He helps people remember to be careful with fire in the woods.

◀ Smokey Bear warns people to be careful around campfires.

A Risky Job

▲ Firefighters in New York City have to fight fires in tall buildings.

Fighting fires is very risky. Some firefighters have to climb very tall buildings. They have to enter rooms that are on fire. They have to be brave. And, they have to know how to stay calm.

Being a firefighter is hard. But, it is also **rewarding**. It feels good to help people when they are in trouble. Would you like to be a firefighter when you grow up?

These firefighters use a ladder to reach the fire.

A Day in the Life Then

Benjamin Franklin (1706–1790)

Benjamin Franklin lived long ago. There were no fire stations where he lived. He wanted to keep the city safe from fires. So, he started a club. It was called the Union Fire Company. Men worked in groups. They tried to stop fires.

Let's pretend to ask Benjamin Franklin some questions about his job.

When did you decide to be a firefighter?

I wanted to be a sailor. My father did not like this idea. So, I became a printer. I love to write. And, I love to help people. I always think of new ideas. The fire company is one of my best ideas. It is a great way to help my community.

What is your job like?

We carry two buckets of water at the same time. The water helps us put out the fires. We have to fill the buckets many times. It is hard work! We do not get paid. Many of us have other jobs, too. We work very long days.

What do you like most about your job?

I think my job is important. Fires can hurt people and their homes. We help keep our city safe. The community is happy with our work. And, that makes me happy.

⬥ Franklin helped cities prepare to stop fires.

Tools of the Trade Then

▲ Fire engines used to look like this. Horses pulled them. They had cans on the back. These cans held a lot of water.

◀ This firefighter is wearing a uniform from long ago. He is also wearing a helmet. It kept his head safe.

▲ Firefighters did not always have hoses. They used to carry buckets of water. It took a long time to put out fires!

Tools of the Trade Now

Some fires are very big. ➤
Helicopters can drop
water from above.
This helps put out big fires.

This is a fire engine ➤
from today. It is big.
And, it goes very fast.
It can carry many tools.

◄ Firefighters use
hoses today.
The hoses spray
a lot of water.
Uniforms are
very special
today. They will
not catch on fire.
This keeps the
firefighters safe.

A Day in the Life Now

Justin Fleming

Justin Fleming is a firefighter. He is also a paramedic. He works in Orange County. Mr. Fleming has been fighting fires for four years.

Why did you decide to be a firefighter?

I like to help people. And, I like to serve my community. I also enjoy riding in the fire engine. I never wanted to be anything but a firefighter.

What is your job like?

I work 24-hour shifts. We exercise (EK-suhr-size) in the mornings. This helps us stay healthy. Then, we train or do **fire inspections** (in-SPEK-shuhnz). We cook lunch and dinner every day. We get about 10–15 **calls** a day. At night, we can study or watch movies. When we go to bed, we still might have to wake up for a call.

What do you like most about your job?

I get to come to work each day and work with great friends. We laugh and have fun. But, we also help people every day. We keep them safe. I like making a difference in their lives.

Glossary

calls—dangerous events that firefighters respond to

crowbars—special tools used to pry things apart

dalmatians—dogs that are strong and fast; they are white with spots

dispatcher—person who calls fire stations to send firefighters out to a fire

fire engines—trucks that pump water with engines

fire inspections—when firefighters check buildings to make sure they are safe

fire station—a building where firefighters work

paramedics—people who help those that are hurt during an emergency

rescue—to save from danger

rewarding—feelings of pride gained from doing something good

shift—hours that a firefighter works in a row between days off

sirens—devices that make loud warning sounds

snorkel truck—a truck with a hose that shoots water high in the air

uniforms—clothes that look the same and are worn by everyone in a group

Index

Credits

Acknowledgements

Special thanks to Justin Fleming for providing the *Day in the Life Now* interview. Mr. Fleming is a firefighter in Orange County, California.

Image Credits